THE **FISH** SERIES

CHRISTMAS

THE BEST OF CONTEMPORARY CHRISTIAN MUSIC

ISBN 978-1-4234-5633-9

HAL•LEONARD® CORPORATION

7777 W. BLUEMOUND RD. P.O. BOX 13819 MILWAUKEE, WI 53213

Visit Hal Leonard Online at
www.halleonard.com

BETHLEHEM'S TREASURE

Words and Music by
BOB FITTS

BETHLEHEM CALLS

Words and Music by EDDIE CARSWELL
and DREW CLINE

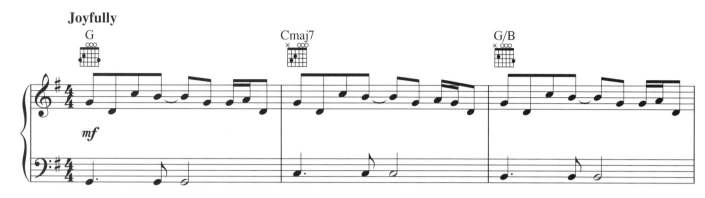

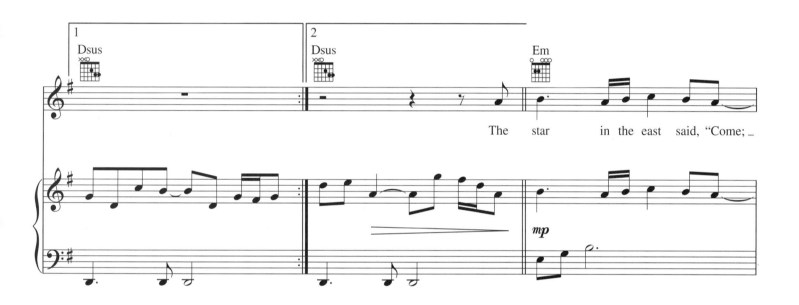

The star in the east said, "Come; the wise men, ev-'ry-one." Heav-en's

come, and let us a-dore ___ Him. _____ ___ Him. _____

BORN TO DIE

Words and Music by JASON INGRAM
and BEBO NORMAN

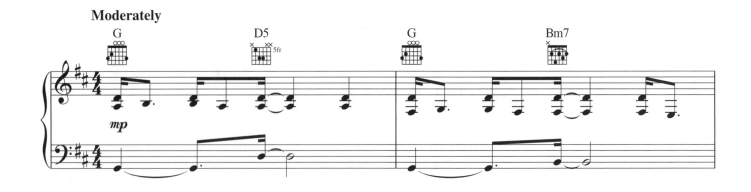

CALL HIS NAME JESUS

Words and Music by
SHAWN CRAIG

CHRISTMAS BLESSING

Words and Music by EDDIE CARSWELL
and MICHAEL O'BRIEN

Male: I re-mem-ber our first Christ-mas; we were young and so in love.

*Recorded a half step lower.

Both: Now here we are, ___ an-oth-er year, an-oth ___ er Christ-mas,

Female: and there's some-thing you should know:

This ___ is my ___ Christ-mas bless-ing, this ___ is my ___ Christ-mas prayer. *Male:* No

mat-ter where ___ the years ___ may take ___ us, love will find ___ us there. ___

CHRISTMAS ANGELS

Words and Music by JONAS MYRIN
and MICHAEL W. SMITH

Joyfully

Christ - mas an - gels sing all a - round __ us, spread good tid - ings o - ver the earth, tell - ing of the Child in a man - ger who is born. He is the __ King of _____

CHRISTMAS IS ALL IN THE HEART

Words and Music by
STEVEN CURTIS CHAPMAN

In a one bed-room a-part-ment on the hum-ble side __ of town, __ there stands a lit-tle Christ-mas tree; it looks a lot like Char-lie Brown's. __ And un-der-neath __ there's one lit-tle gift __ for him, __

CHRISTMAS MAKES ME CRY

Words and Music by
MATTHEW WEST

Moderately slow

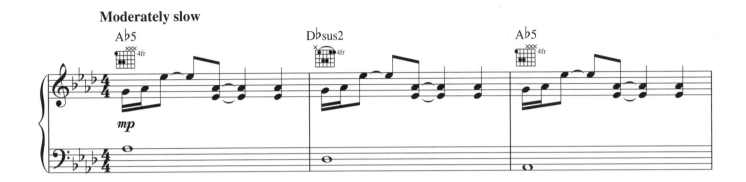

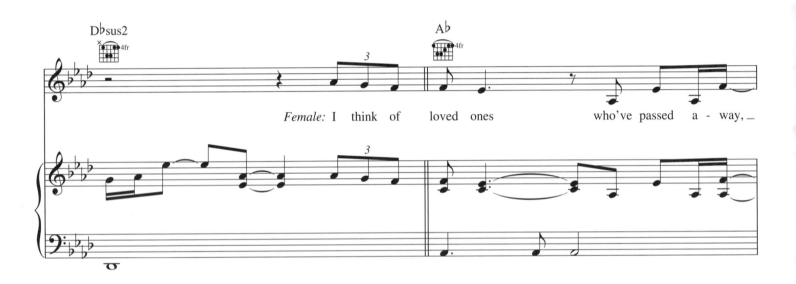

Female: I think of loved ones who've passed a - way,

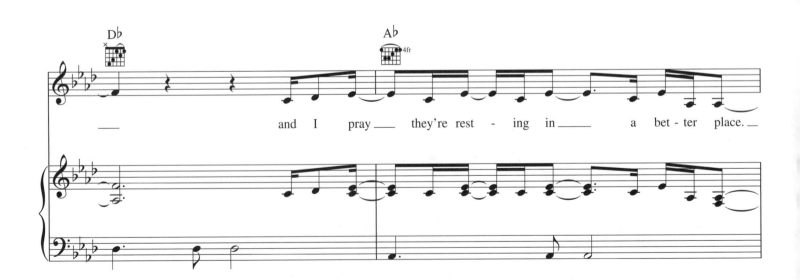

and I pray they're rest - ing in a bet - ter place.

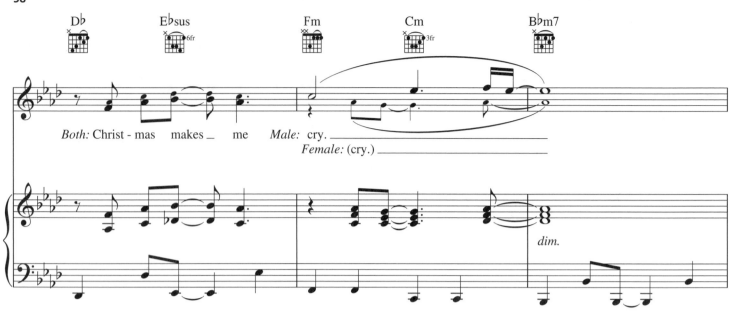

Both: Christ - mas makes _ me Male: cry. _____

Female: (cry.) _____

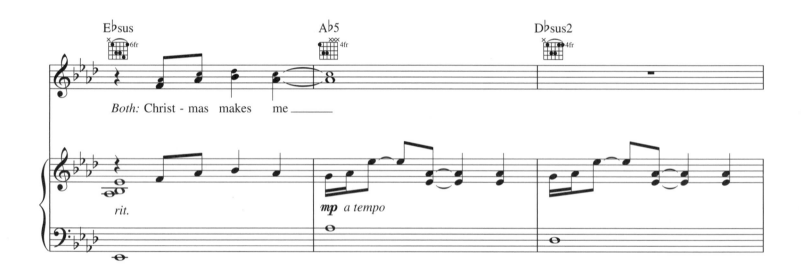

Both: Christ - mas makes me _____

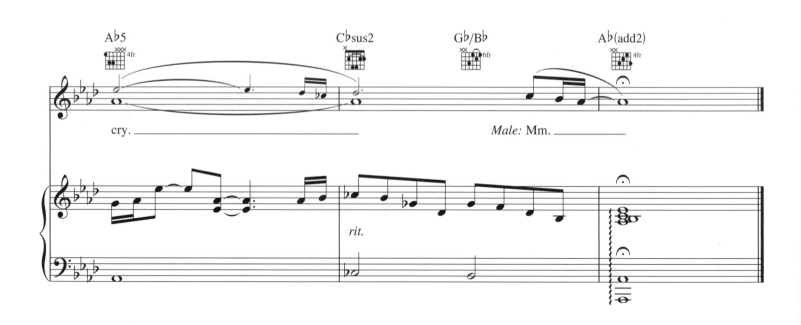

cry. _____ Male: Mm. _____

CHRISTMAS OFFERING

Words and Music by
PAUL BALOCHE

Moderately slow

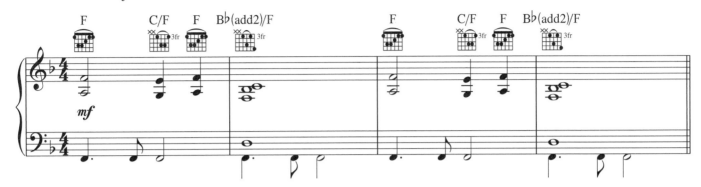

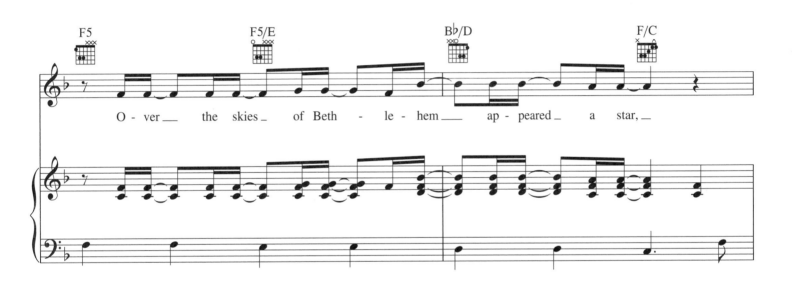

O - ver __ the skies __ of Beth - le - hem __ ap - peared __ a star, __

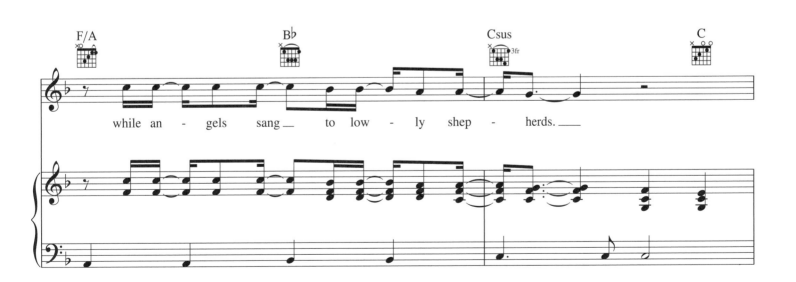

while an - gels sang __ to low - ly shep - herds. __

Three wise men seeking truth traveled from a-far,

hop-ing to find the Child from heav - en.

Fall-ing on their knees, they bowed be-fore the hum - ble

Prince of Peace. I bring an of -

62

64

THE CHRISTMAS SHOES

Words and Music by LEONARD AHLSTROM
and EDDIE CARSWELL

It was al-most Christ-mas time; __ there I stood in an-oth-er line, __ tryin' to buy that last gift or two, __ not real-ly in the Christ-

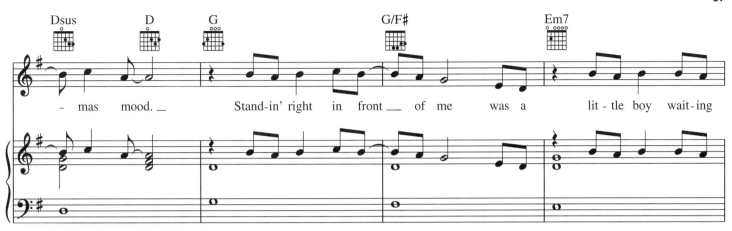

- mas mood. __ Stand-in' right in front __ of me was a lit - tle boy wait-ing

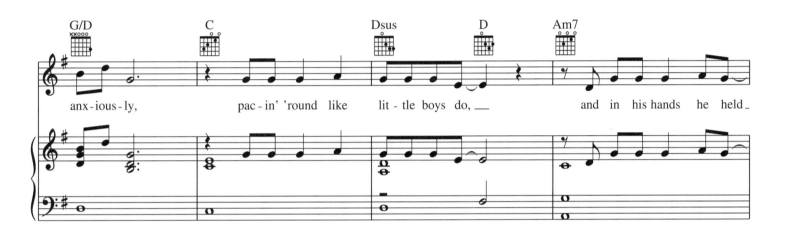

anx - ious - ly, pac - in' 'round like lit - tle boys do, __ and in his hands he held __

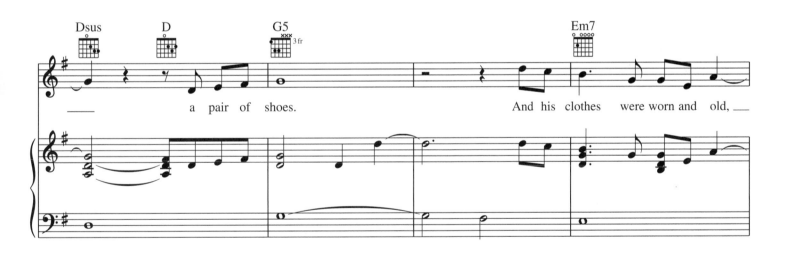

__ a pair of shoes. And his clothes were worn and old, __

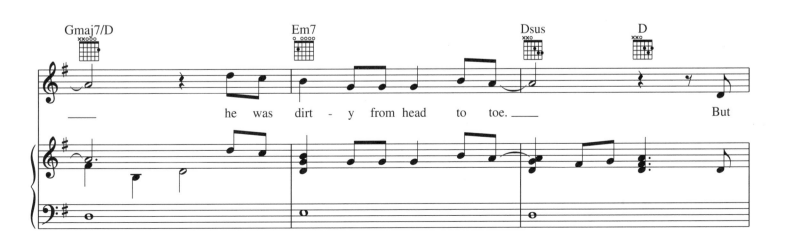

__ he was dirt - y from head to toe. __ But

THE CHRISTMAS STAR

Words and Music by KIMMIE RHODES
and KEVIN SAVIGAR

CHRISTMASTIME

Words and Music by MICHAEL W. SMITH
and JOANNA CARLSON

time is here a - gain!

time is here a - gain!

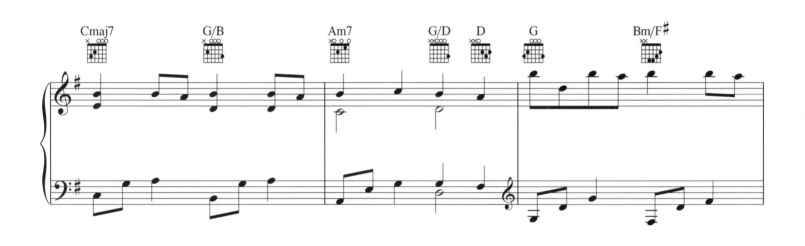

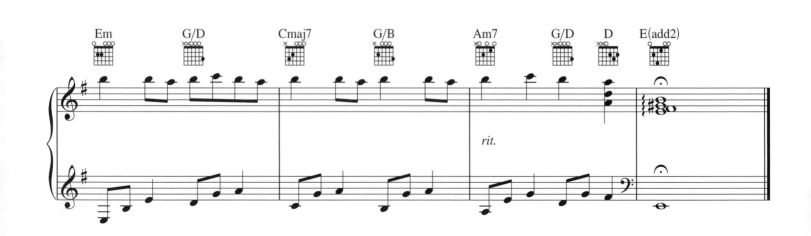

rit.

HOLY LAMB OF GOD

Words and Music by GARY SADLER
and STEVEN TAYLOR

DO YOU HEAR WHAT I HEAR

Words and Music by NOEL REGNEY
and GLORIA SHAYNE

Said the night wind to the lit-tle lamb,
lit-tle lamb to the shep-herd boy,

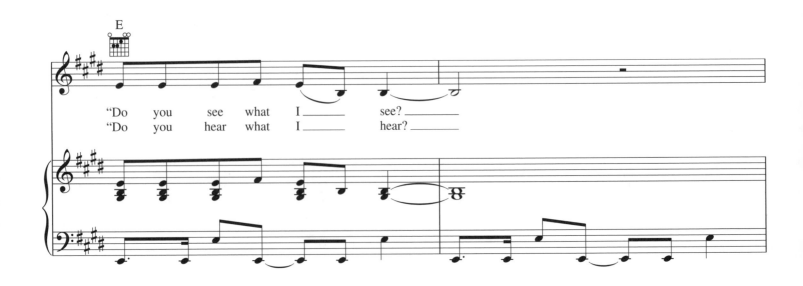

"Do you see what I _____ see? _____
"Do you hear what I _____ hear? _____

HE MADE A WAY IN A MANGER

Words and Music by LEE BLACK
and STEVE MERKEL

Long-ing for ___ a Sav-ior, a
Beth-le-hem, ___ a sta-ble be-

hope-less world ___ would wait. ___ Sin de-mand-ed jus-tice at a
came a throne ___ of grace, ___ as God Him-self, ___ our Sav-ior, drew ___

HEIRLOOMS

Words and Music by BOB FARRELL,
BROWN BANNISTER and AMY GRANT

Up in the at-tic, down on my knees,
Wise men and shep-herds, down on their knees,

life-times of box-es time-less to me.
bring-ing of their treas-ures to lay at His feet.

all that I come from, and all that I live for, and

all that I'm long-ing to be.

My pre-cious {fam-'ly / Sav-ior} is more than an heir-loom to

me.

HERE WITH US

Words and Music by JOY ELIZABETH WILLIAMS,
BEN GLOVER and JASON D. INGRAM

HOLY CHILD

Words and Music by ROB MATHES
and PHIL NAISH

I CELEBRATE THE DAY

Words and Music by
MATT THIESSEN

IT TOOK A CHILD TO SAVE THE WORLD

Words and Music by REGIE HAMM
and GEORGE KING

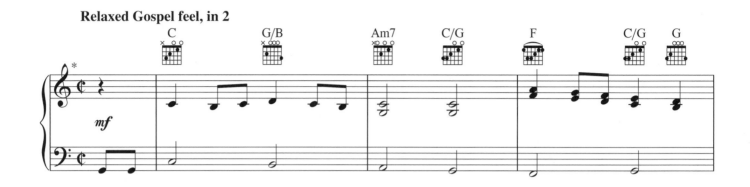

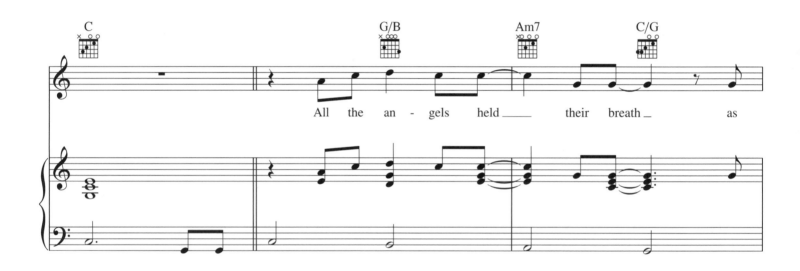

All the an-gels held _____ their breath ____ as

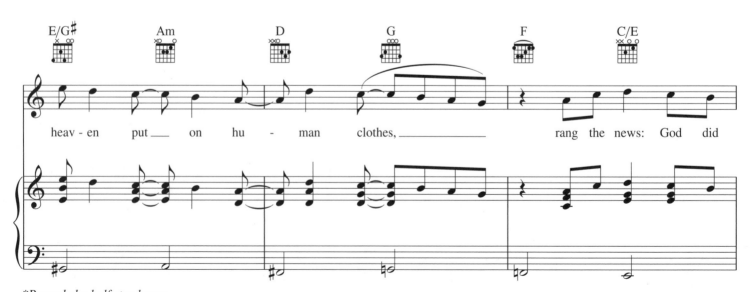

heav-en put ___ on hu-man clothes, _____ rang the news: God did

*Recorded a half step lower.

JOSEPH'S LULLABY

Words and Music by BART MILLARD
and BROWN BANNISTER

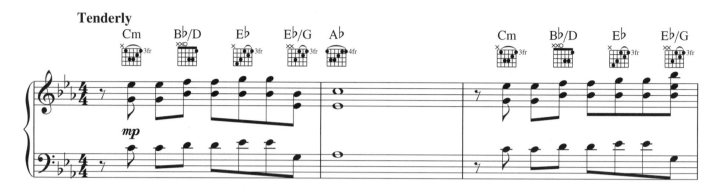

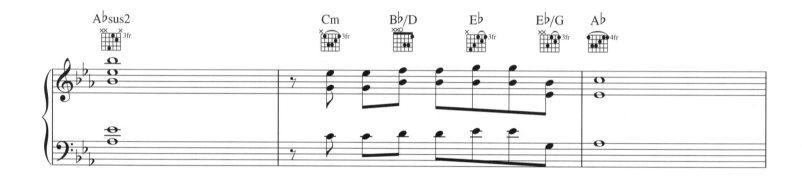

Go to sleep, my _____ son, this
Go to sleep, my _____ son,

A KING IS BORN

Words and Music by SY GORIEB
and TIM HOSMAN

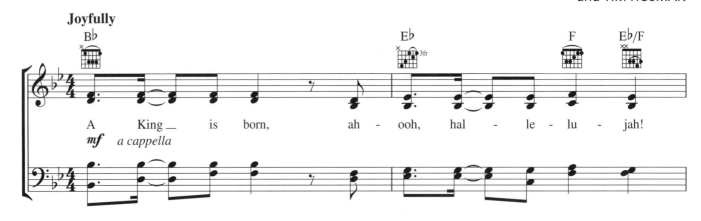

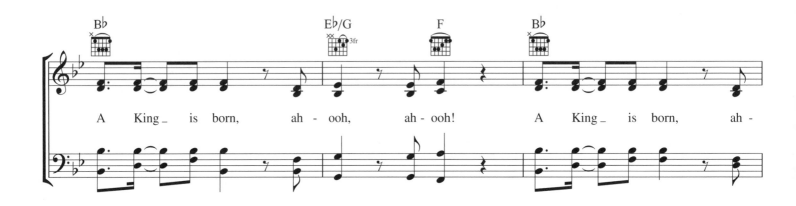

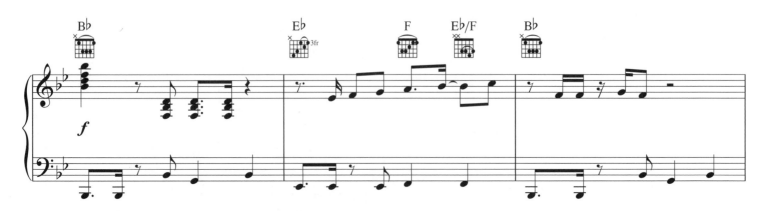

LET THERE BE LIGHT

Words and Music by SCOTT KRIPPAYNE
and MARIE REYNOLDS

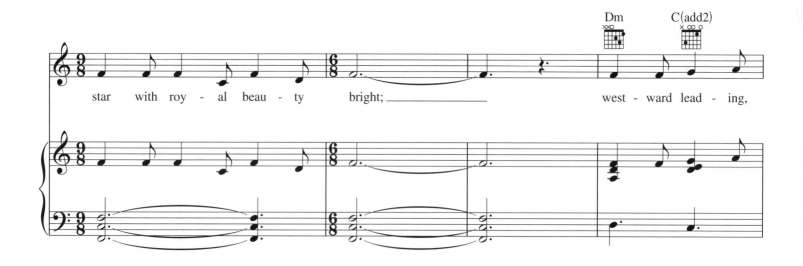

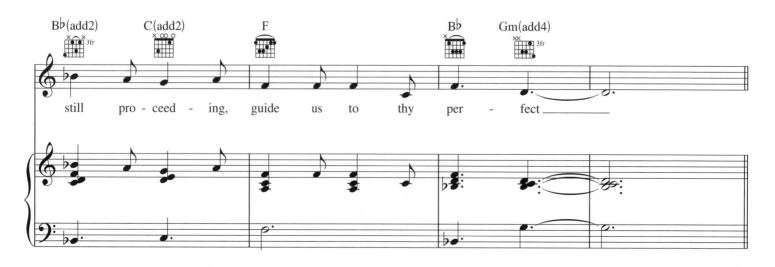

MANGER THRONE

Words and Music by
JULIE MILLER

Moderately slow, in 2

What kind of _ king _ would
left the _ sound _ of

leave _ His throne _ in _ Heav-en to make _ this earth His _ home? _ While
an-gels' praise _ to _ come _ for men _ with un-kind _ ways. _ And

men seek _ fame _ and great re-nown, _ in _ low-li-ness, _ our
by this _ ba-by's help-less-ness, _ the _ pow'r of _ na-tions is

MARY HOLDS THE LIGHT

Words and Music by JOEL LINDSEY
and REGIE HAMM

THE NIGHT BEFORE CHRISTMAS

Words and Music by
CARLY SIMON

NO EYE HAD SEEN

Words by AMY GRANT
Music by MICHAEL W. SMITH

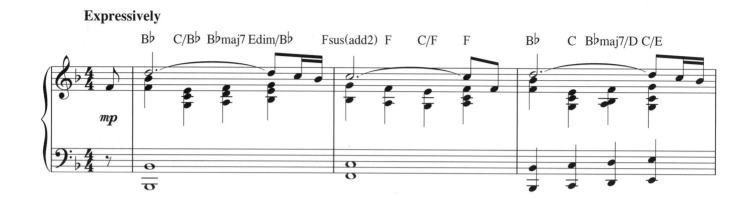

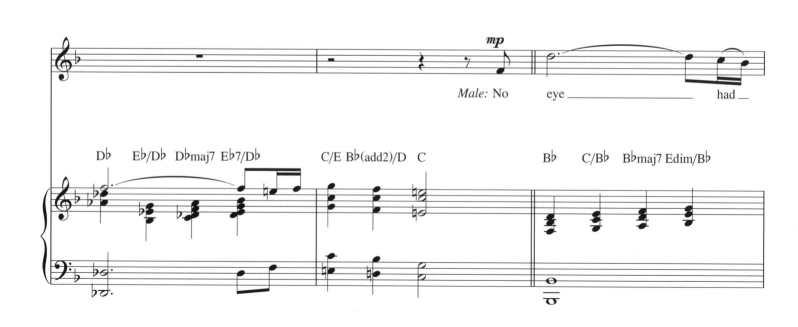

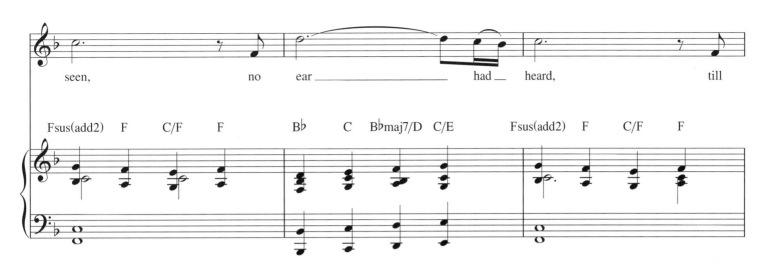

seen, no ear _____ had ___ heard, till

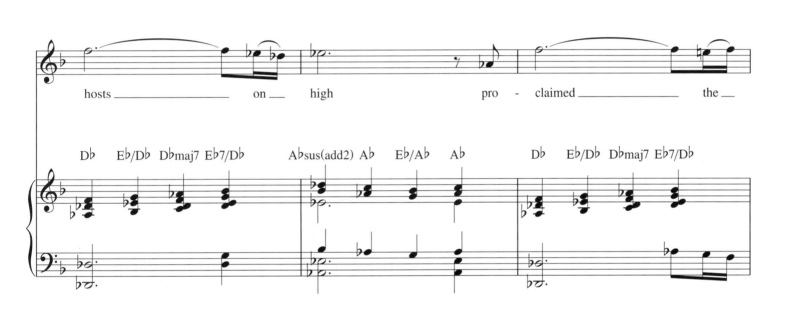

hosts _____ on ___ high pro - claimed _____ the ___

Female: Qui - et - ly, with no one watch - ing,

birth. And heav'n _____ brought ___ down its

NOT THAT FAR FROM BETHLEHEM

Words and Music by JEFF BORDERS,
GAYLA BORDERS and LOWELL ALEXANDER

ONLY ONE

Words and Music by WARRYN CAMPBELL,
ERICA MONIQUE ATKINS-CAMPBELL
and TRECINA ATKINS-CAMBELL

OUR BLESSED SAVIOR CAME

Words and Music by
CARMAN

The an-gels were sum-moned __ by God's __ com-

PERFECT LOVE
(Mary's Song)

Words and Music by RUSSELL FRAGAR
and DARLENE ZSCHECH

UNTO US
(Isaiah 9)

Words and Music by LARRY BRYANT
and LESA BRYANT

Peo - ple ___ who walk in the dark - ness ___ are
boot that ___ who has marched to the bat - tle ___ will

going to ___ be - hold a great ___ light.
fi - nal - ly be set a - flame.

PRECIOUS PROMISE

Words and Music by
STEVEN CURTIS CHAPMAN

Oh, what a pre - cious prom - ise, oh, what a gift __ of love; __ __ an an - gel tells __ a vir - gin that __

SAVIOUR OF THE WORLD

Words and Music by
KATIA BOWLEY

SEASON OF LOVE

Words and Music by HUNTER DAVIS,
GEORGE COCCHINI and CHRIS FAULK

*Recorded a half step lower.

like a row of dom - i - noes. ___

Sea - son ___ of love;

a chance ___ to shine ___ in the dark - ness, to be ___ hope,

to give ___ joy. All o - ver the world, ___ it's Christ - mas.

Christ _ is here _____ with _ us, in our __ hearts,

through our ___ hands. Love is the sea - son.

Vocal ad lib.

Repeat and Fade

Optional Ending

2000 DECEMBERS AGO

Words and Music by JOEL LINDSEY
and REGIE HAMM

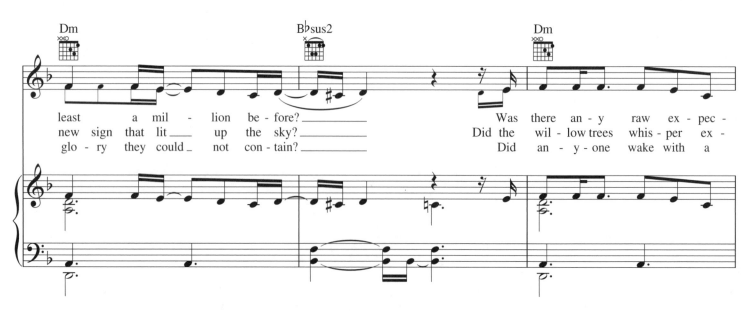

ta - tion, ____ like there was some kind - a some - thin' in store? ____ Did the
cite - ment ____ to the riv - ers and streams __ pass - ing by? ____ Did the
feel - ing ____ of peace that they could __ not ex - plain? ____ Oh, the

sky have to hold __ back the thun - der? Did the moon find new rea - sons to
joy ric - o - chet __ off the moun - tains till it filled up the val - leys be it
love must have been __ o - ver - whelm - ing as it warmed ev - 'ry - one __ in its

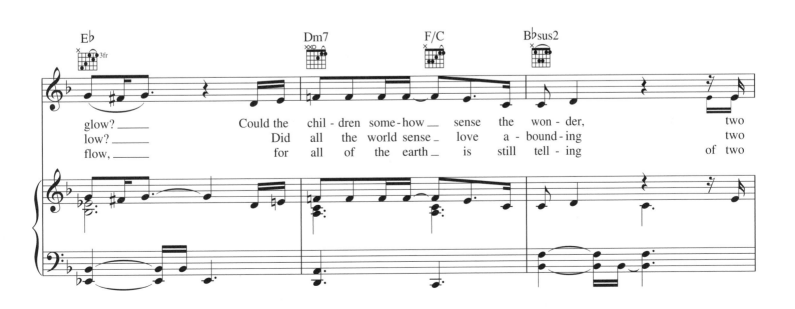

glow? ____ Could the chil - dren some - how __ sense the won - der, two
low? ____ Did all the world sense __ love a - bound - ing two
flow, ____ for all of the earth __ is still tell - ing of two

WHEN LOVE CAME DOWN

Written by CHRIS EATON

WHILE YOU WERE SLEEPING

Words and Music by
MARK HALL

Oh lit-tle town of Beth - le-hem, looks like an - oth-er si - lent night.

YOU ARE EMMANUEL

Words and Music by PAUL BALOCHE
and CLAIRE CLONINGER

YOU GOTTA GET UP
(It's Christmas Morning)

Words and Music by
RICH MULLINS